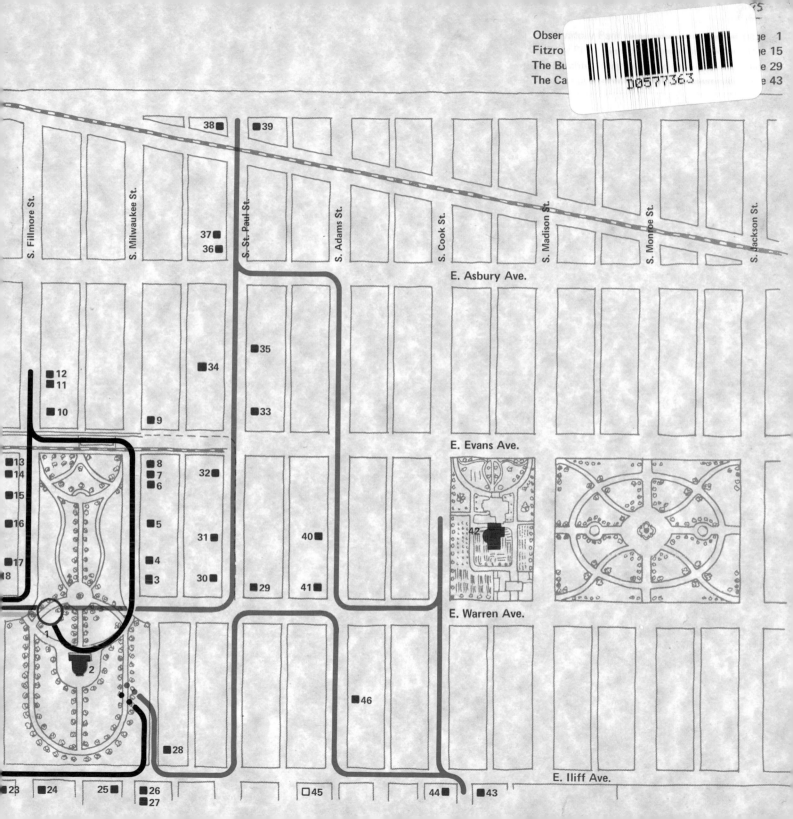

UNIVERSITY PARK

DENVER

Dout Her

for Gregory
and Katrina
who grew up in
University Park
and for Carolyn
who guided them

Four Walking Tours

DENVER UNIVERSITY PARK

*1886-1910
an introduction to the
cultural heritage of
a Denver community*

Written and
photographed
by Don D. Etter

The publication of this book was made possible by the
generous financial support of E. Warren Willard,
the Erik Taylors and the Grassfield family, by
recollections which many University Park residents
were willing to share, and by the cooperation of
the Denver University Library Special Collections staff
and the archivist of the Rocky Mountain Conference
of the United Methodist Church.

Design and Composition/Graphic Impressions

Editorial Assistance/Elizabeth Imig

Printing/The Printing Establishment

Graphic Impressions, Incorporated/Publisher

Four Walking Tours

[96] 2035 South York Street
— demolished, 1973

University Park

University Park was founded, developed and settled as a university town on the prairie, beyond the fringe of settlement in the Denver vicinity. Today, University Park is an urban neighborhood within the Denver city limits— yet "the Park," as it is affectionately called by those who live there, has retained its character as a community.

The following walking tours provide an introduction to the cultural heritage— architectural and social— of the University Park community. The focus of the tours is on the period of 1886-1910, but the early years were only the beginning.

University Park does not have the same national recognition as, for example, the college communities of Hyde Park in Chicago or Cambridge, Massachusetts. Yet there exists in University Park the same opportunity as in those areas— to preserve a small but significant cross-section of our architectural heritage as a part of a viable community. Perhaps more importantly, there exists in University Park the opportunity to maintain the sense of community so often missing in our twentieth century cities.

All tours begin at Observatory Park, 2900 East Warren Avenue at South Fillmore Street (2200 block south). The tours may be taken separately or may be combined.

The numbering of the tour stops is coordinated with the numbering of the photographs and of the site locations on the end paper map of University Park. There is a brief glossary of architectural terms following the last tour stop.

Tie rod anchor

[1]

[2]

Observatory Park Tour

[1] Observatory Park   1886

Observatory Park was one of three parks planned for the University Park area. All three parks were to be laid out with symmetrical walks and gardens. University Park itself was a typical grid pattern of streets extending from what is now South Colorado Boulevard on the east to South Race Street on the west and from East Iliff Avenue on the south to East Jewell Avenue on the north. It should be noted that Observatory Park was not originally bisected by Warren Avenue.

The tour now proceeds to Chamberlin Observatory in the center of the south section of the park.

**[2] Chamberlin Observatory   1888
Robert S. Roeschlaub, architect**

Although the cornerstone of Chamberlin Observatory bears the date 1890, construction on the main building was started two years earlier. The Observatory was a gift to Denver University from H. B. Chamberlin, who was a Methodist, amateur astronomer and wealthy local real estate promoter. It was described by a contemporary English astronomer as "the most perfect astronomical structure on earth." Later, after he had lost his wealth, Chamberlin frequently visited the Observatory. On one occasion he is reported to have told a local resident, "All I have left is what I gave away."

The architect of the Observatory, Robert S. Roeschlaub, was one of Denver's first and possibly its finest nineteenth century institutional architect. His name is carved in stone over the main entry along with the name of the building. Also to Roeschlaub's credit are University Hall [89], the Central City Opera House, Trinity Methodist Church, and numerous Denver public school buildings, including the notable Corona (now Moore) school.

The Observatory is an elegant combination of forms, styles and materials and is one of the few outstanding nineteenth century buildings remaining in Denver. The iron dome was originally complemented by an iron balcony at the second level; slits in the stonework for the balcony supports can still be seen. The juxtaposition of rusticated stonework and painted woodwork is particularly striking. To the west of the main observatory is a smaller building known as the Students' Observatory.

The tour now proceeds northeast to the intersection of Milwaukee Street and Warren Avenue, then north along Milwaukee Street.

[3]

Chimney detail

[4]

[5]

[6]

[3—8] Professors' Row   1887-1898

In the late nineteenth and early twentieth centuries, the 2100 block of South Milwaukee Street was known as Professors' Row. The houses are a cornucopia of late Victorian visual delights. The first three [3,4,5] are still owned by The Iliff School of Theology; the rest [6,7,8] are privately owned.

[3] 2184 So. Milwaukee St.   1887
Grey Gables

One of the most historic structures in Denver, this simple but smartly articulated Queen Anne house was the first University Park residence of the dynamic Methodist-Episcopal Bishop Henry White Warren and his wife Elizabeth, who was the widow of the wealthy Colorado cattle baron, John Wesley Iliff. The Warrens were among those who urged the establishment of University Park as a permanent location for Denver University, and they showed their commitment by pioneering the residential settlement. The great porch with its turned pillars, the shingled second-story bay, the varied roof and gable lines, the paneled verge boards and the chimney brickwork are typical of the style. The carriage house to the rear is one of the few modest examples left in the city and deserves to be preserved for that reason alone. After the Warrens moved to Fitzroy Place [42] they rented Grey Gables to subsequent Denver University chancellors, including Henry A. Buchtel.

[4] 2168 So. Milwaukee St.   1887

Both this house and Grey Gables [3] stood vacant for nearly two years after they were built because of the lack of adequate domestic water. Even after water was available, according to one resident of Professors' Row, jackrabbits far outnumbered people in University Park. The original brick exterior of this house has been painted and the original porch, extending across the front and around the south side, has been removed. The diminutive dormer over the front entry and the larger dormer which cuts into the eave on the north side add variety to the pyramidal roof.

[5] 2142 So. Milwaukee St.   c. 1896
[6] 2118 So. Milwaukee St.   1898

Similar architectural features are employed in these houses—a tent-like roof, an overhanging second story, grouped windows, and brackets—but with surprisingly different results. While both might be described as late Queen Anne in style, the house at 2142 South Milwaukee Street [5] evokes a simple Tudor mood, whereas the house at 2118 South Milwaukee Street [6] follows a more elaborate Swiss-inspired pattern. The front bay at 2142 South Milwaukee Street was carefully executed and the brackets and shingling at 2118 South Milwaukee Street are particularly fine.

[7]

Parlor window

[9]

[8]

[10]

[7] 2112 So. Milwaukee St. 1896
The Kimball House

The Kimball house is a fascinating and pleasing combination of Italianate stylistic elements, which had been popular for decades when it was built, and neo-Federal stylistic elements, which continued to be popular well into the twentieth century. The iron cresting on the roof, the stone lintels and sills, the woodwork of the front window, the chimneys and the brick belt course around the house are features worth noting. For many years George D. Kimball, an early occupant of this house, was associated with the Kimball Red Sandstone Co., which supplied much of the sandstone for the early sidewalks in University Park.

[8] 2102 So. Milwaukee St. c. 1893
The Hyde House

This house was built for the aristocratic Ammi Bradford Hyde, Professor of Greek at Denver University, and his wife Mira. In many ways it might be dismissed as a standard Victorian cottage. However, the original elements which remain visible today set it apart as having been well designed and effectively embellished. The carefully composed woodwork in the gables and the porch pediment, the small lights in the upper windows, and the varied window shapes on the north side all contribute to the overall effect. The original porch contained a half-moon screen and a low railing with turned balusters extending across the entire front. The south chimney is new, but in keeping with the neo-Tudor chimneys common to the era.

[9] 2084 So. Milwaukee St. 1888
The Evans Store

Corner stores were a typical and necessary part of late nineteenth and early twentieth century neighborhoods. This corner store was built by ex-governor John Evans to serve the isolated university community, and the University Park Market was operated here from 1890 until 1968. The original University Park Post Office and the first Sunday School in the Park were also housed in this corner store. Early photographs reveal elaborate gable brickwork and roundels in the south wall. The combination of stone and brickwork lintels over the second story windows is typical of the period. The building has been recently refurbished and once again provides an attractive focal terminus for Professors' Row.

The tour now turns left (west) on Evans Avenue, and then right (north) on Fillmore Street.

[10] 2076 So. Fillmore St. 1905

Projecting, bracketed eaves, a slightly flared hipped roof, and a columned porch were common stylistic elements throughout Denver after the turn of the century in small cottages, modest homes such as this, and some large mansions. The fleur-de-lis tie rod anchor on the south chimney and the paddle brackets under the eaves are characteristic details.

[11]

[13]

[14]

[16]

[15]

[11] 2060 So. Fillmore St.   1909

Exaggerated and bulky front dormers were also common architectural features in Denver during the early years of this century. The corbeled-roof bay on the south side and the shingling and stucco work of the gables of this house are a distinctive combination. The tastefully rehabilitated house at 2052 South Fillmore Street [12] was built slightly later. Further to the north, near the railroad tracks, were the original Denver University playing fields.

The tour now reverses direction and proceeds south on Fillmore Street.

[13] 2105 So. Fillmore St.   1900

The front gable, simple neo-Classical detailing, and broad front porch of this story and a half house are typical of many similar houses built in Denver around 1900. The original red brick has been stuccoed.

[14] 2111 So. Fillmore St.   1892

One of the most attractive facades in University Park, the shingled gable, paneled verge boards, horizontal decorative brick courses and multi-light main window of this house produce a visually stimulating composition. Four roundels on the north side, a beveled glass front door and brickwork of the south chimneys are also notable features. A small stable is visible to the rear.

[15] 2127 So. Fillmore St.   1891
The Honeymoon Cottage

This small, unique cottage is one of the gems of University Park. It was called the honeymoon cottage by early residents because it was often rented to newly married Denver University faculty members. Leaded glass and detailed brickwork add charm to the overall image, and neo-Classical dentils in both wood and brick, as well as the course of pressed bricks in the button design at the front window sill level, are distinctive details. The stoop over the side door is a nice surprise.

[16] 2143 So. Fillmore St.   1909

The simple dignity and timeless appeal of the neo-Federal facade of this house are highlighted by the attractive door frame and pediment.

Front porch detail

[17]

[19]

[18]

[17] 2163 So. Fillmore St.   1890
The Russell House

Modern siding does some injustice to this house, but a few original details can still be seen—a delightful decorative gable, the front porch, the stone foundation and window sills, and the framing around the second-story window of the front gable. Dr. and Mrs. Herbert E. Russell lived in this house from the early 1890's to 1927, and Dr. Russell was considered by many to be both sweet and obstinate, as well as the most popular teacher at Denver University. The Russells' yard, like that of most early University Park residents, was a small farm, and their cow played the key roll in a student prank which consisted of taking the cow into the upper reaches of University Hall [89] and leaving it there for later discovery by the professors. Dr. Russell was killed in 1927 when he refused to abandon his new Pierce Arrow which had stalled in front of an on-coming train at a nearby grade crossing.

[18] 2167 So. Fillmore St.   c. 1891
The Waterbury Cottage

Although the custom of building small cottages at the back of lots has persisted in University Park throughout the years, this cottage is reported to have originally been the carriage house for the Russell house next door [17]. During the late 1890's it became the home of Luther W. Waterbury, long-time employee of the Knight-Campbell Music Co. Later it was occupied briefly by the Henry A. Buchtel family.

The cottage was recently enlarged and attractively stuccoed, leaving little hint of its original shape.

[19] 2201 So. Fillmore St.   1891
The Howe Residence

This substantial and forward-looking home was built for Dr. Herbert Alonzo Howe and his wife Fannie. Dr. Howe was the first Professor of Astronomy at Denver University and Director of the Chamberlin Observatory [2]. In his time, the entire astronomical world was interested in his activities. Dr. Howe was a great teacher, scholar and gentleman. He is reported to have missed the 1910 passing of Haley's Comet when he fell asleep waiting at the observatory telescope.

The Howe house has retained much of its original appearance—particularly the locally produced red-orange brick—and, happily, recent repairs have been consistent with the original design and quality of construction. The quality of this house is particularly apparent from the north—the careful composition of the brick chimney and shingled gable, an art nouveau glass window, and elegant brick belt courses and radiating voussoirs over the windows.

[20]

[21]

[23]

[22]

[24]

[20] 2255 So. Fillmore St. 1907
The Beggs-King Bungalow

Originally built for the Charles and Gertrude Beggs family, this bungalow was for many years the home of Judge Alfred Rufus King, who was appointed to serve on the Colorado Court of Appeals in 1911. The low sweep of the roof, the diamond-paned windows and the heavy brackets of the porch are characteristic bungalow features. The original front windows on either side of the main door have been replaced with modern picture windows.

[21] 2257 So. Fillmore St. 1906
[22] 2273 So. Fillmore St. 1906

During the last years of the nineteenth century and the early years of the twentieth century, the basic plan of these houses was repeated extensively in Denver. The placement of the porch and its embellishments were often the only variants. Both houses have unique gargoyle downspouts on the porch, but only the ones on 2273 South Fillmore Street [22] are easily visible from the walk.

[23] 2305 So. Fillmore St. c. 1909

More than one residence of this design was built in University Park, probably inspired by a plan from a house pattern book. The sweeping roof, horizontal rows of windows and shingle siding are reminiscent of earlier shingle style homes designed by the noted eastern firm of McKim, Mead & White. Dating of structures is often complicated by unexplained discrepancies in otherwise reliable sources, but 1909 is the most probable choice in this case.

The house facing at 2300 South Fillmore Street (1911) [24] is worthy of note because of the charm and effectiveness of a recent rehabilitation.

A number of attractive Edwardian homes and an occasional nineteenth century frame cottage or farm house are located between Iliff Avenue and McWilliams Park. One pleasant unmarked detour proceeds from here south along Fillmore Street to McWilliams Park, returning to Observatory Park on Milwaukee Street.

11

[25]

[26]

[28]

The tour itself proceeds east on Iliff Avenue to Milwaukee Street.

[25] 2950 E. Iliff Ave.   1906
The turn-of-the-century facade of this house has been obscured by recent remodelings, although it is not beyond restoration. Fine brickwork is particularly noticeable in the bay on the east side of the house.

[26] 2300 So. Milwaukee St.   1895
Early photographs of this imposing house reveal a predictable combination of late Queen Anne design features: shingled gables with projecting verges, dramatic roof combs and ridge pole finials, a columned and pedimented porch, and a Palladian window— the only element which has been preserved. The exaggerated sandstone lintels over the main front windows and the tall, narrow shape of the windows themselves form a nice counterpoint. The much remodeled house immediately to the south, 2330 South Milwaukee Street (1906) [27], also had shingled gables, two of which have survived.

The tour now proceeds north on Milwaukee Street.

[28] 2288 So. Milwaukee St.   1898
The Jackson Residence

This solid, red brick house was built to the taste of the well known Quaker physician, Edward Jackson. Quality in construction was emphasized and decorative elements were kept to a minimum. Even the south bay was added after the initial construction. Some of the first plate glass windows in Denver are said to have been part of the original construction.

The tour now returns to Observatory Park across Milwaukee Street.

13

Porch capital and pilaster

[29]

[31]

Fitzroy Place Tour

This tour leaves Observatory Park and continues east along Warren Avenue to the intersection of St. Paul Street. Typical sandstone sidewalks can be seen here and elsewhere in University Park. It is said that Elizabeth Iliff Warren had the first sandstone sidewalk installed on the north side of Warren Avenue from Fitzroy Place [42] to the campus [88] so as to make the way more passable. After a winter snow, Mrs. Warren would direct her driver to harness the Warrens' fine team of horses to a snowplow to clear the walk.

[29] 3109 E. Warren Ave.   1910
The Milligan House

An irregular window grouping, front bay, chimneys and neo-classical details enliven this plain and solid house. The split demi-lune in the gable is an attractive detail. The house was built for Edward W. Milligan, an executive with W. H. Kistler Stationery Co., and his wife, who was Dean of Women at Denver University. The house across the street at 2175 South St. Paul Street (1891) [30] has been remodeled so extensively that only the original shape is apparent. However, the shapes of these two houses illustrate a transition from the predominantly light and vertical articulation of the peaked Victorian cottage to the solid, horizontal lines of the Edwardian house.

The tour proceeds north along St. Paul Street.

[31] 2153 So. St. Paul St.   1907
The Tibbals House

Stately proportions mark this no-nonsense Edwardian house built for the Tibbals family. A simple cube, it is articulated by the outward projection of three flared roofs over the porch, the main house and an attic dormer. The absence of surface decoration is a notable contrast to the embellishment of earlier houses such as the Walter house [32]. However, the Tibbals house is not totally without decoration. The flared chimneys, slightly bowed bay on the south, well proportioned porch pillars and leaded glass window to the right of the front door add a delicate, understated beauty to the house.

[32]

[34]

[35]

[32] 2111 So. St. Paul St.   **1890**
The Walter House
Frederick A. Walter, general contractor

This classic Queen Anne house is among the most romantic and interesting in University Park and is obviously the work of a master designer. The corner tower, which is intersected by the front gable, produces a visually exciting mosaic in combination with the shingled, overhanging upper story and the interplay of textures and decorative elements. The various elements of the house are welded into a unified whole by the regular horizontal repetition of windows and the carefully articulated eave, bracketed second story, window sill and foundation lines. The original porch had heavy balustrades on both sides leading to a brilliantly designed recessed entry which is unique in University Park except for Fitzroy Place [42]. Frederick A. Walter, a general contractor, built and then occupied this house for several years. It has been suggested that Mr. Walter was one of the contractors involved in the construction of Fitzroy Place and that the architect of Fitzroy Place (or at least a draftsman from his office) was responsible for the design of the Walter house—and that leftover materials from Fitzroy Place were used in the construction of the Walter house.

The tour continues north on St. Paul Street. Along the way note the attractively rehabilitated plan-book house at 2076 South St. Paul Street (1912) [33]. Examples of this style can be found throughout the United States, although this particular variant was most widely built in Denver.

[34] 2057 So. St. Paul St.   **1890**

Early photographs reveal that this cottage was originally located next to the Walter house [32]. Reportedly it was first used as a residence by carpenters employed in the building of both the Walter house and Fitzroy Place [42] and later as a residence for the gardener at the Iliff mansion [41]. Modern siding now covers the original clapboards.

[35] 2050 So. St. Paul St.   **1893**

A small window between floors in the south gable and the tower-like room over the front door provide a pleasing contrast to the otherwise simple bulk of this house. The original stick style porch has been removed, but the resulting emphasis on the decorative shingles and other facade features is pleasing.

[36]

[37]

[39]

[38]

[36] 1989 So. St. Paul St.   **1908**

Although somewhat remodeled, this cottage is still a good example of the popular use of red brick and white woodwork in Denver homes of the period. The shingled bell-cast gable, different dormers on the north and south sides, and the summer porch in the back are harmonious features.

[37] 1983 So. St. Paul St.   **1898**

Stepped brick parapets were more often employed in the design of double houses than single residences, as here.

[38] 1901 So. St. Paul St.   **1891**
[39] 1904 So. St. Paul St.   **1891**

These carefully kept frame cottages are among the earliest homes in University Park. They were near the coal yard, nursery and brick yard which served the area in the early years. Oldtime residents tell how their families were able to survive the lean years after the silver crash of 1893 only because the local grocer and the local coal man were generous in extending credit. The nursery was abandoned after a few years, but the young trees and shrubs survived to supply "free for the digging" plantings for the early homes in the Park. A careful search of the area just north of the railroad tracks reveals other early frame cottages.

The tour now returns south along St. Paul Street to Asbury Avenue, then left (east) to Adams Street, then right (south) along Adams Street.

[40]

[41]

South facade

[40] 2145 So. Adams St.   **1899**
The Iliff Mansion

Graceful yet substantial, this red brick home was built for William Seward Iliff (son of John Wesley Iliff) and his wife, Alberta Bloom Iliff (daughter of the cattle and banking Blooms of Trinidad, Colorado). Iliff was largely responsible for the construction of the Denver University stadium (an early reinforced concrete monument now destroyed) and of The Iliff School of Theology [90]. Alberta, one of nine 1897 graduates of Denver University, made her home here until her death in 1967. It was she who, in response to the desires of the University Park community, was instrumental in saving Fitzroy Place [42] from the developers' bulldozer.

The Iliff mansion is of a style which was to dominate much building in Denver during the early 1900's. It is large without being bulky, and the modeled, pagoda-like roofs emphasize the horizontal lines of the house and soften the angularity of the brick. The great curving front porch, the north sun porch, roof combs and brickwork quoins evoke the mood of a pavillion. The carriage house is equally well designed.

[41] 2187 So. Adams St.   **1909**
The Beggs Residence

This fine, symmetrical neo-Georgian house is beautifully proportioned, handsomely finished and one of the best examples of the style in Denver. It was built for Robert H. Beggs, principal of Whittier School in Denver and a trustee of Denver University. Its stuccoed, pedimented gables, fans over the gable windows, central bay over the front porch, small lights in the upper sash windows, and south porch are appropriate to the style.

The tour turns left and proceeds east to the intersection of Warren Avenue and Cook Street.

21

Window grate

Main entry detail

Carriage house

Gardener's cottage

[42]

[42] 2160 So. Cook St.   **1892**
Fitzroy Place
The Warren Residence
Frank E. Edbrooke, architect

Fitzroy Place was built as the permanent University Park residence for Bishop and Mrs. Henry White Warren who moved into Fitzroy Place just 27 years after he completed his service as a Union Army chaplain and 24 years after she first came to Denver, alone, to sell Singer sewing machines. When criticized for spending $50,000 on the residence, Mrs. Warren is reported to have countered with "I spent $100,000." Fitzroy Place was last occupied as a residence by Mrs. Warren's daughter, Louise Iliff, until 1966 when the property was acquired by the Randell-Moore School.

One of the outstanding architects of the time, Frank E. Edbrooke, was chosen to design Fitzroy Place. Edbrooke used conventional materials, methods and motifs in the design, but the result was far from conventional. The magnificent main house is dominated neither by its size nor by its exquisite though limited decoration, but rather by its overall composition, including windows of varying sizes, shapes and positions, Queen Anne towers which are molded into the main structure and a massive roof which unifies the disparate elements of the design. Like the H. C. Brown Hotel (popularly known as the Brown Palace Hotel), also designed by Edbrooke, the Warren residence is both lively and intriguing. Colonial design motifs, present but less noticeable in the main house, dominate the two surviving dependencies, a small, shingle style gardener's cottage and the carriage house. The cottage is one of Denver's few extant shingle style structures and the carriage house, although relatively conventional, is one of Edbrooke's most successful domestic designs.

The tour now proceeds south on Cook Street.

23

[43]

[44]

[46]

[43] 2300 So. Cook St.   1892
The Babcock House

Recently rehabilitated and enlarged, this attractive house is particularly notable for its north porch and handsome corner tower. There are other delightful features as well, such as baroque gable brackets on the north side, which can be glimpsed through the trees. The house itself was built on a terrace above the street, a common Victorian practice which was little employed in University Park. The house was built by John S. Babcock, a substantial early landowner in the area. Like most early residents of the Park, the Babcocks had a vegetable garden irrigated with water carried in small ditches from the High Line Canal. It was he who donated the land where the original University Park School was built in 1892. Only a few early homes remain to the east of the Babcock house.

The tour now proceeds west on Iliff Avenue.

[44] 3334 E. Iliff Ave.   1907

The bungalow, which made its first appearance late in the 1890's, was a popular style for small houses through the 1920's. Many were shingled, as in this commendably remodeled example, and most had low pitched roofs, bracketed eaves and horizontal rows of windows.

The tour continues west on Iliff Avenue. The original University Park School (1892) [45] was located near the intersection of Iliff Avenue and Adams Street. Although structurally sound, it was demolished during the summer of 1973. The tour turns right (north) on Adams Street.

[46] 2254 So. Adams St.   1910

The bungalow is one of the architectural antecedents of the ranch style house which proliferated during the 1940's and 1950's. This well maintained shingled bungalow is a particularly dignified example of a style that was often more rustic in mood. The roof brackets and horizontal rows of windows in the gables are nicely articulated. The original front porch has been enclosed, but in a manner in keeping with the original design.

The tour continues north to Warren Avenue, then left (west) along Warren Avenue, then left (south) along St. Paul Street.

[47]

[48]

Front dormer

[47] 2220 So. St. Paul St.   1905
The Johnson House

An exaggerated third-story dormer dominates this facade and creates an impression of overwhelming bulk. Available records indicate a 1905 construction date, but part of the house may have been built earlier. Red sandstone hitching posts still stand in the parkway. H. E. Johnson, an early owner of this house, was on the staff of Colorado Milling & Elevator Co., one of Denver's pioneer businesses.

[48] 2260 So. St. Paul St.   1905

Elegant neo-Jacobean gables contrast dramatically with the sharp lines of the roofs and windows. This house is presently a single family residence, but was originally built by Henry A. Buchtel as a double house. Each unit was reached from the common front porch and had a living room, dining room and kitchen from front to back on the first floor and three bedrooms on the second floor. The brickwork design between the two main front windows was a common architectural feature of the day. The bungalow to the south at 2280 South St. Paul Street (1911) [49] is a good example of a style variant which dominated the architecture of many modest Denver homes during succeeding years.

The tour continues south along St. Paul Street, then right (west) along Iliff Avenue to Observatory Park.

27

[50]

Main facade detail

[52]

[53]

North facade

The Buchtel Neighborhood Tour

This tour leaves Observatory Park and continues west along Warren Avenue to the intersection of Clayton Street and then proceeds right (north) on Clayton Street.

[50]   2181 So. Clayton St.   1902
The Shattuck House
attrib. William E. Fisher, architect

A truncated roof and dropped eave were used in an effort to minimize the height of this house and accent its strong horizontal lines. Well sited and with considerable presence, the house was a gift to Mr. and Mrs. Hubert L. Shattuck from her father, a Eureka, California rancher and banker. Mr. Shattuck was the son of the Joseph C. Shattucks, early University Park residents. The yard of this house and that of the much later stately residence to the north at 2157 South Clayton Street [51] contain a number of beautiful specimen trees.

[52]   2140 So. Clayton St.   1891

This well kept cottage, one of the earliest and most enchanting homes in University Park, typifies what many people have come to think of as pure Victorian. The different shapes of decorative shingles, the eyebrow hoods in the gable and over the upper-story window, and the sunburst panel in the porch pediment are an outstanding composition.

[53]   2122 So. Clayton St.   1890
The Cutler House

For over 70 years this house has been the residence of the Cutler family. Ira E. Cutler, a Connecticut Yankee, was a science professor at Denver University from 1898 to 1935. His interests ranged well beyond his academic work, however, for he was a painter, choir director, and horticulturist. It was through Dr. Cutler's efforts and encouragement that many varieties of trees were planted in University Park and on the Denver University campus. Indeed, trees planted by Dr. Cutler virtually obscure the house today, revealing only glimpses of the attractive shingling and panel work. On the north side an interesting square motif is repeated in the small window lights, the gable woodwork, and the horizontal brick courses. Decorative shingles and frame supports in the gables add to the variety of the facade.

The porch and south summer room were added by the Cutlers after they purchased the house in the late 1890's. Dr. Cutler acquired two of the lots to the south of this house in lieu of salary when Denver University experienced financial difficulties following the 1893 silver crash.

29

[54]

[55]

[56]

[57]

[54] 2114 So. Clayton St.   1910
attrib. F. T. Adams, general contractor

Several houses in University Park are attributed to Fred T. Adams, who acted as both designer and builder. He often took his plans from pattern books or architectural publications, making modifications to suit the desires of his clients. Numerous variations of this conventional Edwardian house exist in University Park as well as elsewhere in Denver. In addition to this house, the Buchtel and Roberts bungalows [66, 67] are firmly attributed to Adams. The Miles bungalow [79] and the house at 2260 South St. Paul Street [48] also show evidence of his hand.

[55] 2111 So. Clayton St.   1910

Comfortable-looking and transitional, this house anticipates the bungalows of the next decade.

[56] 2073 So. Clayton St.   1906

Bold dormers dominate this modest house and give it a startling and forceful appearance. The precast pebble panels in the front dormer were typical of the period, but are seldom in evidence today.

[57] 2061 So. Clayton St.   1901

Neo-Classical details, decorative shingles, a leaded glass window and a side bay enhance an otherwise simple design.

The tour continues north and then turns left (west) at Asbury Avenue. At the northeast corner of Asbury Avenue and Columbine Street is the site of the first girls' dormitory in University Park, Wycliffe Cottage [58], now demolished. The northwest and southwest corners of this intersection were originally planned as a park [59]. The tour turns left (south) on Columbine Street.

31

[60]

[63]

[65]

[60] 2018/20 So. Columbine St. 1897

This double house is a simple cube embellished with a pedimented porch. Regency-inspired decoration on the neighboring house at 2026 South Columbine Street (1900) [61] is intriguing, but is from a later remodeling. At 2055 South Columbine Street is another double house (1901) [62].

[63] 2075 So. Columbine St. 1906

Although founded in 1894, University Park Methodist-Episcopal Church did not own a parsonage until it acquired this house. The side bay and the placement of upper story windows near the corner of the house are unusual features. Across the street at 2072/74 South Columbine Street (1906) [64] is a small double house; the variegated brickwork of the facade has been obscured by a recent coat of paint, but the surface patterns, tie rod anchors and stepped gable are still very much in evidence.

The tour now detours left (east) a half block on Evans Avenue.

[65] 2525 E. Evans Ave. 1886

At this address is the first house built in the Park. Although often called the Dyer House, after Father John L. Dyer, the "snowshoe itinerant" who supposedly once lived there, it was actually built by J. A. Clough, president of the Colorado Savings Bank and a Denver University trustee, and was first occupied during the summer of 1886 by a Mr. Bray who "looked after" the Park. For the present it is these historic associations which make the house important, for architecturally it is undistinguished and much remodeled. It is interesting to speculate as to which parts of the house were built at different times. Complete restoration, of course, would require converting East Evans Avenue into rural lane, reuniting the two halves of the neighborhood.

The tour now reverses directions, returns to Columbine Street and continues left (south).

Main entry

[66]

[67]

[66] 2100 So. Columbine St.   1905
The Buchtel Bungalow
F. T. Adams, general contractor

Chancellor and Mrs. Henry Buchtel started the foundation of this "modern bungalow" in 1905, and one of the escutcheons on the lamp pedestals originally bore the Buchtel name. They had previously lived at Grey Gables [3] from 1899 until 1901 when, after the death of their son, Henry Jr., they moved first to the Waterbury cottage [18] and then to the President's house [86].

Like its owner, the Buchtel bungalow was in its time vigorous, independent and forward-looking. It now provides early evidence that architecutral styles were by then moving east as well as west, for the style is based in part on early California bungalows. The massive brackets, originally painted brown, and the "white" brick were both new to the Denver scene. When Henry A. Buchtel was elected governor of Colorado in 1906, he continued to reside in University Park and the Buchtel bungalow served as the governor's mansion during his two year term.

Buchtel is also associated with a number of other important local buildings. As a Methodist minister he preached his first Denver sermon in the Evans Chapel [93] and was pastor of Trinity Methodist-Episcopal Church during construction of the present church at 18th and Broadway. During the construction of Trinity Church, Reverend Buchtel climbed the scaffold to lay the mortar and place the cross on the steeple top. He came to Denver University in part to help put it on a sound financial basis and it was during his administration, and in large measure due to his efforts, that Science Hall, the Carnegie Library [94], Buchtel Memorial Chapel [95] and the gymnasium [98] were constructed on the Denver University campus. He and Mrs. Buchtel took a personal interest in the design of these buildings as well as in the design of their bungalow. After Dr. Buchtel's death in 1924, Mrs. Buchtel agreed to sell the bungalow to Denver University at a "modest" price, knowing "that if the University owned this house she and [Dr. Buchtel] would always be a part of this cherished place."

[67] 2112 So. Columbine St.   1905
The Roberts Bungalow
F. T. Adams, general contractor

Less startling than the Buchtel bungalow but even more advanced architecturally is this bungalow built at the same time for the Frank H. H. Roberts family. It is reminiscent of residences designed by Frank Lloyd Wright during the prior decade. Salient bungalow features include the low sloping roof, bracketed eaves, central dormer and a horizontal, ground-clinging design. The front walls swing outward to accentuate the horizontality of the house. The design of this bungalow should be compared with a similar house at 2266 South Columbine Street [79].

35

[69]

[68]

[70]

[71]

[68] 2124 So. Columbine St.   c. 1890

Stucco now covers this late Victorian house, thus obscuring the red brick walls and sandstone lintels and window sills. Nevertheless much of the original charm is apparent. The basic plan as well as the embellishments are much the same as those of the Cutler house [53]. Arched windows in the south bay are pleasing decorative features, but most intriguing is the absence of the then very common sitting porch. The result is very much like an urban street house.

[69] 2131 So. Columbine St.   1903

Beautifully maintained, this neo-Colonial house illustrates the very effective combination of a then popular style with Denver's ubiquitous red brick. The intersecting lines of the roofs, bays and chimneys, particularly on the north side, are handled with considerable ingenuity. At least three patterns of decorative shingles were used on the siding.

[70] 2135 So. Columbine St.   1896

The basic plan of this comfortable house was used throughout Denver during the late 1890's and early 1900's. However, this particular house is possibly the most elaborate, refined and carefully articulated remaining example. Flared eaves of the hipped roof, modeled shingling of the front dormer, diamond pane windows, the south bay, and the neat balustrade across the front porch all contribute to the overall effect. Similarities to the much larger Iliff mansion [40] are striking.

[71] 2160 So. Columbine St.   1889
The Miller House

A wooden stick style porch originally extended across the front and around the south side of this house. The present front porch changes the mood of the house from romantic to substantial, yet it is not entirely out of keeping with the original design. The three front gables, decorative shingles and the heavy sandstone belt course which bisects the front windows are the dominant features of the original facade.

This house was the home of Mr. and Mrs. W. P. Miller for two decades. Mrs. Miller was one of the first purchasers of lots in University Park, and it was Mr. Miller, a Denver Union Water Co. executive, who made arrangements for University Park to have a permanent water source and for Mr. W. W. Evans to open the University Park Market in the Evans store [9]. When University Park was dedicated on Arbor Day, 1886, Governor John Evans made the major address from Mr. Miller's carriage.

Across the street at 2153 South Columbine Street [72] is a small cottage built in 1903 as the Pi Beta Phi Lodge and since enlarged. It was not a residence since the university authorities did not then permit young girls to live in a house, even with a house mother. At 2174 South Columbine Street [73] is a solid house built after 1910, but nevertheless Edwardian in style. The house at 2181 South Columbine Street [74] was built in 1896 and, although drastically altered since then, still has substantial restoration potential.

37

[75]

[76]

[77]

[78]

[75] 2215 So. Columbine St. 1891
The Ling House

The imaginative design of this house is not repeated elsewhere in University Park. The house was occupied for many years by Charles J. Ling, an early teacher at Manual Training School in Denver. The straight lines of the three gables contrast to the arch of the two main windows, and the shingling of the upper story contrasts with the plain surface below.

[76] 2221 So. Columbine St. 1906

This house is plain but very appealing. Paddle brackets under the eaves and decorative, pressed brick rain lips over the lower windows are worthy of note.

[77] 2233 So. Columbine St. 1909
The Engle Residence
W. D. Engle/R. R. Houghton, designers
R. R. Houghton, builder

If the Victorian houses of University Park can be categorized they would be called romantic, whereas the Edwardian houses, of which this is an outstanding late example, would be called substantial. Happily, the red brick of this house has not been painted, thus allowing a much better image of how houses of this style originally looked at the time it was built for Wilbur and Emma Engle. Dr. Engle was among the loyal band who remained on the Denver University faculty in the years following the silver crash of 1893. The Engles lived first in the Honeymoon Cottage [15] and then in the Walter House [32] before building this residence.

[78] 2255 So. Columbine St. c. 1897
The Chancellor's House

Acquired by Denver University about 1922 and substantially remodeled for a chancellor's residence, this house was originally built for Wilbur and Rose Steele. Mr. Steele was a professor at both Denver University and The Iliff School of Theology. The dignified neo-Federal embellishments were added during the remodeling and make the house one of the most elegant in the Park.

[80]

[79]

[82]

[81]

[79] 2266 So. Columbine St.   1907
The Miles Bungalow

Here is perfect evidence of why the bungalow style caught the imagination of twentieth century Americans. Classic in its symmetry, the house nevertheless has the informal appeal of a cottage. Its horizontal lines are accentuated by curvilinear wings; the urn pedestals on either side of the front entry are a decorative device much used by Frank Lloyd Wright during the late 1890's and early 1900's. The house was originally built for William E. Miles, an executive of The Gano Co., "men's outfitters."

[80] 2301 So. Columbine St.   1908

While the bungalow style swept the country from west to east shortly after 1900, the stucco style moved from east to west. The Mediterranean influence on this style is apparent in the key features of this example—the use of colorful tiles, long sweeping roof lines, horizontal rows of windows and stuccoed walls.

The tour now proceeds east on Iliff Avenue to Clayton Street.

[81] 2300 So. Clayton St.   1901

Key features of the bungalow style are combined with the red brick and white woodwork pattern so familiar in Denver. The classic bungalow was said to require a fieldstone chimney, which perhaps inspired the use of rough brick for chimneys.

The tour now proceeds north along Clayton Street. Along the way note 2217 South Clayton Street [82] which was built in 1911. It is one of the most graceful and inviting homes in the Park. At Warren Avenue the tour either turns right (east) and returns to Observatory Park or turns left (west) to commence the campus tour.

[83]

Bay window and gable

Stained glass window

Parlor window

[84]

The Campus Tour

The campus tour leaves Observatory Park and continues west along Warren Avenue to the intersection of Josephine Street and then turns right (north).

[83]   2180 So. Josephine St.   1890
The Allen House

An outstanding example of a modest late nineteenth century street house, this home incorporates many Queen Anne features. Every detail was carefully exccuted and is in complete harmony with the whole. Leaded glass over the main window and in one of the north windows, a shingled neo-Tudor bay in the front gable and the brickwork in the south chimney are both typical and beautiful. The house was built for John D. Allen, an early Denver watchmaker and jeweler.

[84]   2170 So. Josephine St.   1892
The Evans-Campbell House
Charles A. Cunningham, carpenter

W. W. and Sarah Evans, who came to the Park in 1890, moved into this home after living for two years in the upstairs of the Evans store [9]. Evans operated the University Park Market in the Evans store until his death in 1915. Sarah Evans was appointed postmaster of University Park in 1890 and served in that capacity while the Post Office was in the Evans store. Subsequent to her death in 1934, the house passed to members of the Campbell family. The main front window is a simple but elegant decorative feature, as is the small window to the left of the front door.

[85]

[86]

Bracketed eave

[85] 2161 So. Josephine St.   1907

The combination of a square window and arched window in the facade of this otherwise plain, hipped-roof Edwardian house is both amusing and unique.

[86] 2100 So. Josephine St.   c. 1897
The President's House

The house has served a variety of uses, including that of residence for a president of The Iliff School of Theology and a university commons and boarding club. The tent-like roof, double chimneys (originally single) at both ends of the house, and the steeply pitched overhanging eaves are important features. Early photographs reveal unpainted brick walls and a recessed second-story porch without the more modern superstructure. The effect was very much like a country English manor house. Across East Evans Avenue at 2080 South Josephine Street is Templin Hall (c.1908) [87], originally built as a Denver University dormitory.

The tour now returns along Josephine Street, turns right (west) at Warren Avenue and then continues west to the campus of Denver University and The Iliff School of Theology [88]. One early plan for the campus called for a playground, botanical garden, meandering ponds, an aquarium and a maze. The ultimate result is much more conventional. The tour first proceeds to University Hall on the north side of the esplanade.

[89]

Main entry detail

Main entry column and capital

[90]

[89] University Hall 1890
Robert S. Roeschlaub, architect

Roeschlaub's bold University Hall stands sentinel over the campus like a great castle. It is one of the few remaining nineteenth century Denver buildings of the Richardsonian Romanesque genre and one of Denver's too few remaining architectural and historic landmarks. The outstanding strength of University Hall is the massing of voluminous shapes under the great tent-like roof, originally articulated by a heavy roof comb. However, the details of its facade were not neglected. The color, texture and arrangement of the stone, the varied fenestration, and the carved stonework all contribute to the success of the building. The windows in the two south towers follow the interior stairs while the windows in the two north towers are arranged to match interior rooms. The power of the facade can best be felt by standing at the foot of the main entrance stairs and looking up.

University Hall originally housed all of the University's functions on the University Park campus, from a gymnasium in the basement to literary societies on the fourth floor. Roeschlaub also designed the University's nearby Chamberlin Observatory [2] and a number of other important nineteenth century institutional buildings in Denver.

The tour proceeds south across the esplanade to The Iliff School of Theology.

[90] The Iliff School of Theology 1892
attrib. Frank E. Edbrooke, architect

One of the most graceful nineteenth century architectural compositions remaining in Denver can be seen in the north facade of this distinguished building. Happily, it is in excellent condition. Its architect, Frank E. Edbrooke, worked with identifiably Gothic and Romanesque forms and decorative motifs and with a then conventional massing arrangement, but it is the overall impact rather than the style which gives the building its life. A walk around the building reveals a variety of windows, stone and copper finials on the roof and gables, and an occasional surprise, like the bell lantern on the south roof. The school itself was originally endowed by Elizabeth Iliff Warren in memory of her first husband, John Wesley Iliff, whose son William Seward Iliff contributed handsomely toward the construction of this building. Like University Hall, The Iliff School of Theology is a significant architectural and historic landmark. Edbrooke also designed Fitzroy Place [42], the University Park residence of Bishop and Mrs. Henry White Warren, and a number of other architecturally significant buildings.

The tour now proceeds west around the south side of the Mary Reed Building (1932) [91] and then west through The Mary Reece Harper Humanities Gardens (1965) [92].

47

Memorial window

Roof comb, buttress and entry porch detail

[93]

West facade

[93] Evans Memorial Chapel 1874

This simple High Victorian Gothic chapel was originally constructed at West 13th Avenue and Bannock Street in Denver and was moved to its location on the campus in 1960. Happily, it is near a site originally planned for a chapel. Features of particular note include the soft color of the sandstone, a shingled roof, iron cresting along the ridge pole, the stone cross at the peak of the east gable, and chimney pots which surmount the buttresses at the northeast and southeast corners of the chapel. Some of the numbers painted on each stone to facilitate accurate reassembly on the Denver University campus can still be seen. The memorial window, as well as the pale and lovely painted side windows, can best be seen from inside.

Evans Chapel was spared demolition in 1960 and moved to its present location under the leadership of a small group which, through the then Denver University Chancellor Chester M. Alter, voiced a "growing and understandable concern over the destruction of the homes and churches and other places where Americans before us lived and worked, structures in which are mirrored their way of life, their ideals and character, which are our greatest heritage." Even in its original location the chapel had important connections with University Park. It was constructed by Governor John Evans, a founder of Denver University and of University Park, as a memorial to his daughter, Josephine; Bishop Matthew Simpson, namesake for Simpson's Grove, one of the original parks in University Park, presided at the dedication of the chapel in 1878; Henry White Warren and Elizabeth Fraser Iliff, both long-time University Park residents [3,42] were married there in 1883; and Henry A. Buchtel, Denver University Chancellor and Colorado Governor, preached his first Colorado sermon there in 1884.

The tour now returns east through the Harper Humanities Gardens [92] and north of the Mary Reed Building [91] to Carnegie Library [94].

South entry
before remodeling

[94]

Brickwork detail

[95]

[94] Carnegie Library 1908
R. S. Roeschlaub & Son Co., architects

Now a campus bookstore, this building has been much abused in recent years and the elegant entryway, including brilliant beveled glass, is now partly obscured. However, the building still evokes the pattern of small-town Carnegie libraries long familiar to the American scene.

The tour continues past the Carnegie Library [94] and then turns left (north) and proceeds to the north side of Buchtel Memorial Chapel [95].

[95] Buchtel Memorial Chapel 1907
Thomas Barber, architect

Although started in 1907, Memorial Chapel was not completed and dedicated until 1917. Described as "Moorish Baroque" in style, it is concrete evidence of the wide variety of early architecture to be found in University Park. The architect is reported to have denied designing the building.

From the north porch of Memorial Chapel can be seen the site of one of the most elegant and graceful late Queen Anne residences in the city. This residence [96] was demolished in 1973. A photograph of the facade appears at page vi. Like many nineteenth century University Park homes, this house was located within one or two blocks of the original campus. This area has experienced considerable growth in the last few decades and, as a result, many early homes have been demolished.

The tour now proceeds east, passing Margery Reed Hall (1928) [97] to the left (north) and the gymnasium (1908) [98] to the right (south), before leaving the campus and crossing University Boulevard.

[99] 2116 So. University Blvd. 1900

This small house and the neighboring house to the north at 2112 South University Boulevard (1898) [100] were built for speculation by John Babcock, an early resident of the Park [43]. They are typical of many small houses built in Denver during the late 1890's and the first decade of the twentieth century.

From here the tour proceeds south on University Boulevard.

[101] 2140 So. University Blvd. 1908

Unlike many late nineteenth and early twentieth century neighborhoods, more than two or three homes of a single pattern were rarely built in University Park. Even then, the variations were often substantial. This house and the companion house at 2130 South University Boulevard (1910) [102], are an interesting example of this practice.

The tour continues south on University Boulevard. At 2266 South University Boulevard is the Chamberlain cottage [103], built in 1891, occupied for many years by Curtis Chamberlain, a draftsman, and subsequently much enlarged and remodeled. Continuing south, the tour turns left (east) on Iliff Avenue. On the northeast corner of Iliff Avenue and Josephine Street, 2284 South Josephine Street (1912) [104] is a house built from the same pattern as those at 2130 and 2140 South University Boulevard [102,101]. The tour continues east on Iliff Avenue to Observatory Park.

Balustrade

Bay

Bay window

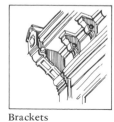
Bellcast gable

Brackets

Bracket

Clapboard siding

Corbeling

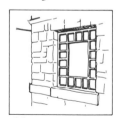
Course

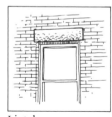
Cresting

Demi-lune window

Dentils

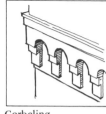
Dormer

Gable

Hip roof

Lights

Lintel

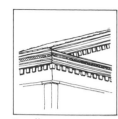
Palladian window

Pediment

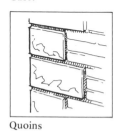
Quoins

Roof comb and finials

Rusticated stone

Shingles

Sill

Stepped parapet

Roundel

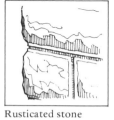
Tie rod anchors

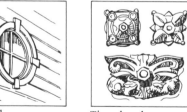
Verges projecting, plain

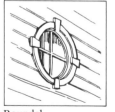

Verge board

Voussoirs

Glossary

Unfamiliar architectural terminology has been avoided in this book. However, readers may find these pictorial definitions helpful.

This brief glossary was adapted from the extensive and useful Canadian Inventory of Historic Buildings prepared by the National Historic Sites Services, Ottawa, Canada. Drawings by Gene Junk.

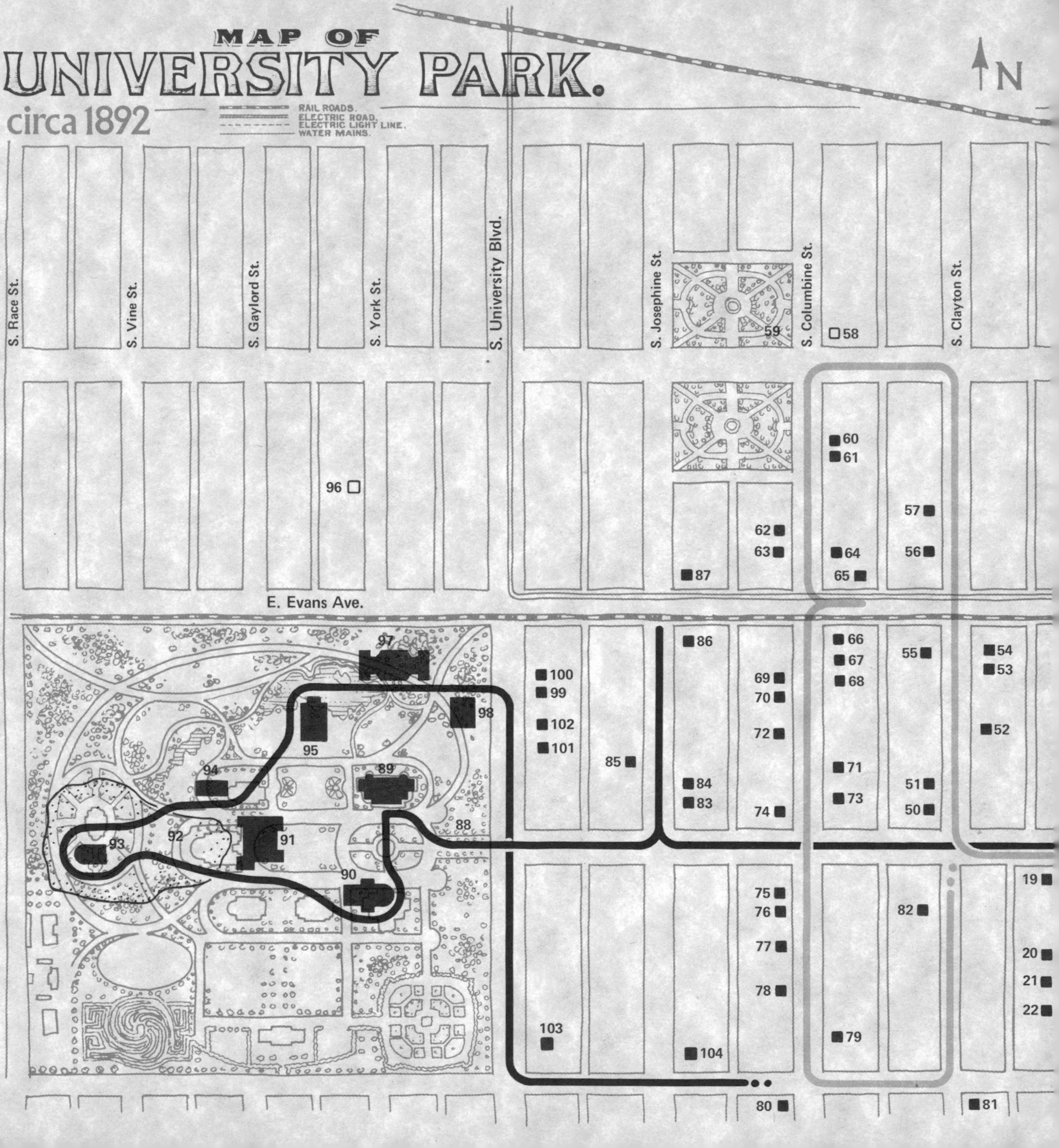

MAP OF
UNIVERSITY PARK.

circa 1892

RAIL ROADS.
ELECTRIC ROAD.
ELECTRIC LIGHT LINE.
WATER MAINS.

N

S. Race St.

S. Vine St.

S. Gaylord St.

S. York St.

S. University Blvd.

S. Josephine St.

S. Columbine St.

S. Clayton St.

59

□58

96 □

60
61

57

62
63

64

56

87

65

E. Evans Ave.

97

86

66
67
68

55

54
53

100
99

69
70

52

102

72

101

71

95

85

94

89

84
83

73

51
50

93

92

91

88

74

90

75
76

82

19

77

20

78

21

22

103

79

104

80

81